BOSTON
THE BEST DOG EVER...

ROBERT NUNN

Copyright © 2024 Robert Nunn

All rights reserved. No part of this book may be reproduced or transmitted in any form or by any means, electronic or mechanical, including photocopying, recording, or by any information storage and retrieval system, without permission in writing from the author.

Boston likes breakfast time…

He loves to lie under the table while his family is eating!

Boston loves going up to the lake...

He loves to go for a ride on the paddleboard!

Boston loves car rides...

He really likes to go for a ride with Grandma in her convertible!

Boston loves going to the dog beach...

He loves to retrieve the stick that is floating in the water and run back to his owner.

Boston goes for a ride in the pickup truck...

He just loves riding in the back of the truck.

Boston loves to visit Grammy and Grandpa at their house...

He takes a warm sunbath and rolls on the grass.

Boston loves to take car rides in the family car...

He sticks his head out the window into the wind
and his ears fly in the wind!

Boston goes camping with his family...

He loves sleeping in the tent with everyone.

Boston likes to sit out in front of the house
when the family is gone...

He is busy guarding the house.
When his family comes home, he howls in delight!

Boston loves dinner time...

He gets to eat the food that gets dropped from the high chair. Boy does he love the extras from the baby!!

Boston loves hugs from his family...

Boston, the very best dog ever!
We love you Boston!

In memory of Boston…

There stands Boston proud and stately
Always on guard to keep everything safely…

He was loved and adored by all who knew him
And as for other dogs he was always kind to them…

And we always used to call him our baby boy
When he was just a young puppy, we would always give him a treat and a toy…

And now that he has gone away, we will never ever be the same
But we promise you Boston, we will never forget your name!

We love you Boston!!!

www.ingramcontent.com/pod-product-compliance
Lightning Source LLC
LaVergne TN
LVHW072123060526
838201LV00068B/4961